American Moments

ABDO
Daughters

THE KENT
STATE TRAGEDY

By Rachel A. Koestler-Grack

VISIT US AT
WWW.ABDOPUB.COM

Published by ABDO Publishing Company, 4940 Viking Drive, Suite 622, Edina, Minnesota 55435. Copyright © 2005 by Abdo Consulting Group, Inc. International copyrights reserved in all countries. No part of this book may be reproduced in any form without written permission from the publisher. ABDO & Daughters™ is a trademark and logo of ABDO Publishing Company.

Printed in the United States.

Edited by: Melanie A. Howard
Interior Production and Design: Terry Dunham Incorporated
Cover Design: Mighty Media
Photos: AP/Wide World, Corbis, Kent State University, John Filo

Library of Congress Cataloging-in-Publication Data

Koestler-Grack, Rachel A., 1973-
    The Kent State tragedy / Rachel A. Koestler-Grack.
        p. cm. -- (American moments)
    Includes index.
    ISBN 1-59197-934-X
    1. Kent State University--Riot, 1970 (May 4)--Juvenile literature. 2. Kent State University--Students--Political activity--History--20th century--Juvenile literature. I. Title. II. Series.

LD4191.O72K64 2005
378.771'37--dc22
                                                                                    2004062298

CONTENTS

THIRTEEN SECONDS

Tension affected many students at Kent State University in Ohio on May 4, 1970. A weekend of riots had caused destruction both on and off campus. The Ohio National Guard now patrolled the streets to keep order. Reserve Officers' Training Corps (ROTC) student William Schroeder said to a friend, "It feels like we're walking through a war zone, rather than going to class."

Elsewhere on campus, Allison Krause prepared for a noon rally. She was excited to participate in a protest against the troops on campus. Her close friend wasn't as enthusiastic as Krause. She admitted, "I'm afraid something might really happen at the rally." "Don't be afraid," Krause reassured her. But she then added, "I'm a little scared, too."

For the first time all quarter, Doug Wrentmore decided to cut his noon English class. He thought the rally would be more interesting. At first, the rally was uneventful. Then the guardsmen tried to break it up.

By 12:20 PM, the situation had reached a crisis. Guardsmen aimed their guns at the students. Wrentmore later recalled, "I decided that things were getting much too dangerous for me. I've never had a gun pointed at me before, so I started to leave." He then heard a sound like firecrackers. He turned around to see what was happening.

National Guardsmen fire
tear gas into the crowd
at Kent State University.

Students dive to the ground and take cover behind cars in Prentice Lot as guardsmen open fire.

Suddenly, he fell to the ground. Looking at his leg, Wrentmore realized that he had been shot.

Jeffrey Miller was closer to the guardsmen. He was one of many students yelling and cursing the troops. It seemed to him like the guards retreated. He turned to a friend and said, "We really showed them that time." Moments later, Miller dropped to the ground in a pool of blood. He had been shot in the face and killed.

After taking an ROTC test, Schroeder headed to a friend's dormitory. He could hear the crowd chanting, "Pigs off campus!" The minute Schroeder heard gunshots, he dove to the ground. One of the stray bullets struck him in the back. He later died.

Sandra Scheuer was on her way to class when the shooting broke out. In order to get to her class, Scheuer had to walk right through

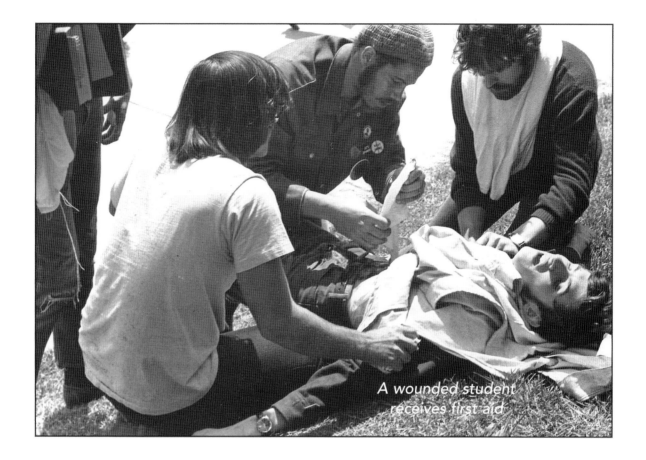
A wounded student receives first aid

the crowd. She, too, was hit. The bullet went through her neck. She fell to the ground dead.

Krause and her boyfriend, Barry Levine, ducked behind a car when the shooting started. As soon as the gunfire ended, Levine turned to Krause. He was relieved that they were safe. But Krause whispered, "Barry, I've been hit." At first, Levine did not believe her. Then he saw blood running from under her arm. He immediately began to scream, "Ambulance, ambulance!" But it was too late.

The shooting went on for only thirteen seconds. Four students died that day, and nine others were wounded. One young man, Dean Kahler, was paralyzed for life. Years after the tragedy, many continue to ask why this terrible event happened.

THE WAR COMES HOME

Although no one is certain what caused the shootings, the protests at Kent State began because of the Vietnam War. After World War II, France ruled Vietnam. Between 1946 and 1954, Vietnamese leader Ho Chi Minh led a revolution against France and won independence. Vietnam was then split into two countries, North Vietnam and South Vietnam.

The United States supported the democratic South Vietnam. But Ho Chi Minh governed North Vietnam as a communist state. U.S. leaders did not want to see communism spread. They saw it as a threat.

Ho Chi Minh wanted to unite Vietnam under a communist government. He attacked South Vietnam. South Vietnam was not strong enough to protect itself from Minh's army or guerrilla fighters. The United States sent advisers to help South Vietnam. U.S. involvement in the war increased after North Vietnam fired on the U.S. ship *Maddox* in the Gulf of Tonkin in 1964.

President Lyndon B. Johnson claimed that another boat was attacked soon after,

Ho Chi Minh

8

THE COLD WAR

U.S. involvement in the Vietnam War was to some extent a result of the Cold War. After World War II, the United States and the Soviet Union developed a rivalry. Both tried to prove that their political and economic systems were superior. This rivalry resulted in the space race, which led to the moon landings. The contest also caused many in the United States to fear and distrust communism.

A U.S. soldier escorts a Vietcong rebel in Vietnam.

In the Vietnam War, the Soviet Union and communist China supported North Vietnam. The United States, in turn, pledged its support to South Vietnam to keep communism from spreading. In this way, Vietnam became a Cold War battleground.

At the height of the Cold War, the Soviet Union installed missiles in Cuba. This sparked the Cuban missile crisis in 1962. The Cuban missile crisis was the closest that the United States and the Soviet Union came to war during the Cold War. Eventually, the Soviet Union withdrew its missiles from Cuba.

The Soviet Union collapsed in 1991, effectively ending the Cold War. By this point, the conflict had spanned more than 40 years.

but this turned out to be false. Nevertheless, Congress passed the Gulf of Tonkin Resolution allowing Johnson to send American troops to South Vietnam. In 1965, Johnson did so.

The communist forces, or Vietcong, were difficult to fight. They used guerrilla tactics. In this method of fighting, groups of soldiers make surprise attacks. The Vietcong hid in the thick forests of Vietnam. Guerrilla fighters also dug tunnels beneath villages and dressed in the same clothes as civilians. U.S. soldiers had trouble finding the guerrilla fighters. They had no way of knowing which people were Vietcong fighters and which were civilians. As the war unfolded, many Americans believed the United States was fighting a war it could not win.

Universities all across the United States held teach-ins to protest the Vietnam War. During these seminars, teachers educated students about U.S. involvement in Vietnam. Teach-ins spread to more than 100 colleges and sometimes involved protest rallies.

Many Americans became excited when President Richard M. Nixon announced that troops would begin withdrawing from South Vietnam in 1969. But six months later, a draft lottery was introduced. This action meant that all men between the ages of 18 and 26 should be ready to go to war if needed.

Then on April 30, 1970, President Nixon announced that U.S. troops would invade Vietnam's neighboring country of Cambodia. Until this time, Cambodia had tried to keep a neutral position in the Vietnam War. However, many believed that North Vietnamese forces were hiding in Cambodia. The bombing was sure to bring Cambodia into the war. This made people think the war was spreading, not ending. U.S. citizens against the war were outraged.

President Richard M. Nixon announces that U.S. forces will invade Cambodia.

RIOT ON NORTH WATER STREET

On Friday, May 1, newspapers headlined the president's decision to invade Cambodia. This news frustrated many Kent State University students who were opposed to the war. Early Friday morning, some unhappy young people spray-painted messages on sidewalks around the university. The antiwar messages included "U.S. out of Cambodia."

Around noon, the Victory Bell located in the middle of campus rang. The bell was taken from an old Erie & Lackawanna train, one of the many trains that ran through the center of Kent. Standing only three feet (one m) off the ground, the bell could be rung by anyone. The resounding gong echoed across campus, calling students to gather.

Over the years, students had rung the bell to call meetings, demonstrations, and peaceful protests. This time, politically-minded Tom Dubis wanted to speak to students about the invasion of Cambodia.

As soon as a crowd gathered, Dubis gave a speech about Nixon's decision. Nixon had ordered troops into Cambodia without the approval of Congress. Dubis claimed that by this act, Nixon was "murdering the Constitution." The highlight of this meeting was to

— THE VICTORY BELL —

University president George A. Bowman had the Victory Bell placed in Kent State Commons in 1950. The bell was donated to the university by the Erie Railroad. Initially, the Victory Bell was rung for Kent State athletic triumphs. It was later used to call together political protests. After the Kent State shootings, officials attempted to remove the bell from the Commons. However, student opposition was so strong that the bell was returned.

bury a copy of the U.S. Constitution. The protest was completely legal and nonviolent.

That night, students gathered at the downtown bars. It was a typical Friday night in Kent. Students dressed in vests, beads, and miniskirts. The warm spring evening brought a heavy crowd to the bars on North Water Street. Many young people gathered around television sets to watch the fourth game of the world championship basketball play-offs. The New York Knicks led the series two to one against the Los Angeles Lakers. Most students wildly cheered for the Lakers to tie the series.

At about 10:00 PM, someone lit firecrackers out in the street. People left the bars and went outside to see what was happening. Just then, someone threw a bottle at a passing car. The bottle shattered one of the rear windows.

A little while later, an elderly couple tried to drive down North Water Street. The people were crowded so thick in the street that the car had trouble getting through. The driver gently nudged one of the students in front of him with his car. The crowd reacted angrily. They smashed the car's windows and began violently rocking the car. The couple finally made it through the crowd and sped away.

Shortly after midnight, police arrived on the scene. All around them, students were screaming and throwing bottles. The protesters had lit a large bonfire in the street. They screamed, "Pigs off the street! We won't go to Cambodia!"

Police ordered that the bars be closed. Students who were inside peacefully watching the basketball game were forced to leave. Customers blamed police for ruining their evening. These angry

Lakers team member Wilt Chamberlain goes in to make a basket during the playoff game against the New York Knicks on May 1, 1970.

students spilled into the streets and joined the other protesters. The crowd moved down the street. They vandalized local stores. Crowd members smashed windows and spray-painted antiwar messages on the walls.

Kent mayor LeRoy Satrom arrived and shouted the riot act through a bullhorn. But the protesters refused to disperse. Fearing the crowd was too dangerous, police fired tear gas into the crowd. This gas caused the students to choke and cough, and it made tears stream from their eyes. Finally around 2:30 AM Saturday morning, the students returned to the campus.

Some Kent State students were ashamed of the destructive protesters. The next day, they brought buckets and brooms to North Water Street and swept up broken glass. But other students continued to cause trouble. They set off false fire alarms and called in prank bomb threats.

Mayor Satrom became increasingly angered by the events. He received reports that carloads of protesters were arriving from Chicago, Illinois, and other cities. Though these reports were not entirely accurate, Satrom feared antiwar demonstrators would start violent riots. He called Ohio governor James Rhodes in Columbus. If Saturday night protesters moved downtown again, the situation could get out of control. He wanted to make sure the National Guard would help him if needed.

GOVERNOR
JAMES A. RHODES

Ohio governor James Rhodes

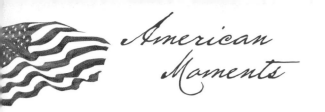

BURNING THE ROTC

Around 7:00 PM on Saturday, May 2, a crowd of young people gathered in the university Commons. Some of the crowd had no connection with the university. These visitors were dedicated antiwar activists who came to protest. Others simply wanted to see what was going on.

The crowd's leaders wanted to burn down the ROTC building. The Kent State ROTC building had been an antiwar protest target for years. On Saturday, it became one again.

As more students filled the Commons, protesters handed out leaflets condemning the ROTC and explaining why it should be destroyed. By 7:30 PM, the crowd grew to more than 600 people. University officials became nervous at the size of the protest. Worried the students would soon cause trouble, they called the Ohio State Highway Patrol for help. The patrol refused to come. Until arrests were necessary, the patrol felt it was a useless trip.

Shortly after 8:00 PM, protesters began chanting, "Down with the ROTC!" The mob of about 2,000 students and protesters rushed toward the ROTC building. They hurled rocks through the windows. A few protesters tossed lit flares at the building. But they failed to set the building on fire.

National Guardsmen walk past the remains of the ROTC building at Kent State.

Students refused to give up. Flares continued to sail through the air. Some protesters set fire to gasoline-soaked rags and threw them through the broken windows. Finally, some curtains burst into flames. The crowd cheered as thick smoke rolled out of the windows. "Burn, baby, burn!" they chanted.

Firefighters quickly arrived on the scene. They had trouble pushing their way through the mob. Several firefighters tried to hook up a hose to a nearby fire hydrant. But protesters grabbed the hose and ran away.

The hose that firefighters were able to hook up didn't last long. Students slashed it with knives and ice picks. Firemen who tried to extinguish the blaze were pelted with rocks. Protesters beat one fireman with a wooden club. For their own safety, the firefighters gave up and left the campus.

University officials once again called the highway patrol. This time, the patrol responded. Shortly after 9:00 PM, the highway patrol and two police units arrived. Meanwhile, Mayor Satrom called in the National Guard.

By 10:00 PM, the ROTC building was consumed by fire. The firemen returned, this time protected by a dozen police officers. But it was too late to control the fire. Inside the building, 1,000 rounds of ammunition began exploding. Students quickly retreated a safe distance away.

The National Guard arrived around 10:30 PM. By this time, the ROTC was almost completely destroyed. The guard announced over large bullhorns, "Ladies and gentlemen, go back to your dormitories.

The Ohio National Guard protects the ROTC building.

If you remain outside, you will be arrested. We do not want to arrest you." Students gradually returned to their rooms. However, the next morning, the missing ROTC building was not the only way Kent State University had changed.

TRAGEDY ON BLANKET HILL

Students awoke on Sunday, May 3, to see the National Guard posted around campus. It almost seemed to students that Kent State University was being invaded. Leaflets made by student body president Frank Frisina and university vice president Robert Matson were also posted. This "special message to the University community" stated that Governor Rhodes and the National Guard were in control of the campus.

The announcement went on to say that all demonstrations were prohibited and that a curfew was in effect. Students had to be indoors between 8:00 PM and 6:00 AM in the city, and between 1:00 AM and 6:00 AM on campus.

Despite these changes, the mood at the university was relaxed. In fact, many people later described it like a carnival. Most students were polite to the officers. Throughout the afternoon, the guards and the students engaged in pleasant conversation. Some of the guardsmen were college students themselves.

Allison Krause noticed one young guardsman in particular. He stood with the butt of his gun on the ground in front of him. A flower stuck out of the barrel. She saw another guard storm over to

A guardsman mingles with students on Sunday, May 3.

him and tell him to pull the flower out. Krause snapped, "Flowers are better than bullets."

At 8:00 PM on Sunday, students led another rally on the campus Commons. The meeting was another protest of the U.S. invasion of Cambodia. The rally started peacefully. But guardsmen worried it would turn violent.

Around 9:00 PM, the guards read the riot act and asked students to go home. Again, students refused to leave. Guardsmen used tear gas to try to break up the protest. Instead of going home, some students participated in a sit-in near the campus gate. As they sat in the street, students sang antiwar songs such as "Give Peace a Chance."

The National Guardsmen tried to move the crowd. The protesters suddenly became hostile. They screamed curses and threw rocks at the guardsmen. Again, the officers used tear gas on the protesters. As violence grew, the guards jabbed into the crowd with bayonets, wounding several students. By midnight, the mob had dispersed.

On Monday, May 4, classes at Kent State resumed as usual. The troops still occupied the campus. If it hadn't been for the troops, few people would have believed the events that had taken place over the weekend. But many students had not forgotten. Some prepared for another rally at noon.

The rally started peacefully. A few hundred students gathered around the Victory Bell. Shortly after the rally began, a university patrolman and three guards circled the Commons in a jeep. One of them announced over a bullhorn that the rally was unlawful. He ordered them to break it up. Some protesters began throwing rocks at the officers. Guardsmen responded by firing tear gas. The troops then began marching toward the students, trying to force them out of the Commons. Students reluctantly retreated.

Guardsmen continued to sweep across the Commons. They drove the protesters to an area of campus called Blanket Hill. The crowd grew to about 1,000 as classes ended and students filed out of the

This photograph taken by John Filo is probably the most famous image of the Kent State shootings. Mary Vecchio is kneeling over the body of Jeffrey Miller. Filo won a Pulitzer Prize for this photograph.

buildings. The troops pushed them down the slope of the hill to the practice football field.

At the bottom of the hill, the guards found themselves boxed in on two sides by chain-link fences. The students were in front of them. Although not surrounded, the only way out of the corner was retreat. A retreat would make it seem as though the students had won. The guardsmen continued firing tear gas to keep the crowd a safe distance away.

Soon, the tear gas began to run out. For ten minutes, the troops stayed on the field, trying to decide what to do. They needed to get back up the hill, where hundreds of students were now blocking their path.

Finally, the guardsmen began marching with their bayonets fixed. Many students quickly scattered. Some students were bolder. They cursed at the troops and held up their middle fingers. Others began throwing rocks, bricks, and empty tear gas canisters. One student ran in front of the marching troops, waving a black flag of protest.

At the top of Blanket Hill, students continued to throw rocks and taunt the guards. The troops later stated they thought they were in danger. A line of guardsmen lowered to one knee and lifted their rifles. One guard fired a warning shot into the air. This sound started a chain reaction. Suddenly, a string of gunfire let loose. Thirteen seconds later, four Kent State students lay dead or dying. Nine others were wounded.

The deafening gunfire stopped. Sounds of screaming and crying then filled the air. Students called for ambulances. Others shouted at the guards to shoot them, too. This went on for almost an hour while

A student throws a tear gas canister back at the guardsmen.

the National Guardsmen gathered at the burnt-out ROTC building. They knelt in a defensive circle with their guns ready.

Professor Glenn Frank finally grabbed a bullhorn. He was choking back tears. "I don't care whether you've never listened to anyone before in your lives," he said. "I am begging you right now. If you don't disperse right now, they're going to move in, and it can only be a slaughter. Would you please listen to me?" The students listened. They walked away in small groups.

SEEKING ANSWERS

One question immediately rose after the shooting: Why did the guardsmen fire? The soldiers claimed their lives were threatened. However, the closest student shot was standing 60 feet (18 m) away. Most of the other students were more than 300 feet (90 m) away. From this distance, the unarmed students could do no real harm to the soldiers. Photographs later showed that only a handful of students were throwing rocks at the time of the shooting. The majority of these stones never even hit the guardsmen.

For years, some people have blamed a conspiracy for the shootings. They think Governor Rhodes and President Nixon may have planned the shooting and later covered it up. Nixon was fed up with all of the antiwar protesters, whom he called bums. Some people thought this event was his way of discouraging more riots. Others thought the guards had poor leadership, and the soldiers were confused. There is also a chance that a small number of guardsmen planned together to shoot the protesters.

People nationwide were shocked by the shootings. But the reaction of the public at the time may seem surprising. Many Americans believed the students got what they deserved. Some people even said all the protesters should have been killed that day. A number of the

To the Rioters, arsonists, Killers of Decency & Sanity.

To the rioting, destrctive, arsonists of colleges buildings window breaking goons, ROTC objectors and saddest of all that you the destructive arsonists ARE the murderers of the four students of your college. It was your actions that are and were responsible for their deaths. Dissenting is one thing but burning and destroying and throwing missles like bottles, bricks, cement chunks etc can kill as well as bullets. The National Guard did not come to Kent college on their own volition but on demand from your President of the college who called for help when the campus police were unable to stem you riotious destructive burning goons. And it is you rioters who are responsibel for forcing the Guard to protect their lives from your violence. Also a bullet in one of the students did not come from a Guardsman's gun so their claim they WERE SHOT AT BY some or manyothers was factual. Shut down your colleges as tax payers want it very much. We are disgusted to pay taxes for college rioters.

One of theAmany millions of disgusted tax payers

The shootings brought out strong emotions on both sides.
This letter is addressed to the student body president at Kent State.

protesters' parents told their children that they, too, should have been shot.

Neither the police nor university officials telephoned the parents the day that their children were shot. Most found out from reporters, radio announcements, or college roommates. Worse, the parents of the victims soon began to receive a large volume of hate letters. These letters called even the dead students traitors and communists.

Students at other colleges were strongly affected by the shootings. The Kent State tragedy triggered student protests at hundreds of colleges across the country. Students rioted and hundreds of universities closed.

Classes did not resume at Kent State until the summer. In the meantime, dedicated professors set up classes off campus or allowed their students to finish classes by mail. On campus, the Federal Bureau of Investigation (FBI) immediately began to look into the shootings.

At first, the guardsmen who shot into the crowd had claimed that a sniper had fired upon them. The FBI tried in vain to find evidence to support this story. In June 1970, the FBI completed its investigation. The findings were sent to the U.S. Justice Department's Civil Rights Division for review.

Attorney Robert Murphy read the FBI's materials and wrote a report for the attorney general. Murphy recommended that the National Guardsmen be charged with violating the civil rights of the protesters.

The Justice Department, however, decided to move the controversial case out of its hands. Responsibility for the case was transferred to

JACKSON STATE

Campus shootings occurred elsewhere besides Kent State. Ten days after the Kent State tragedy, students at Jackson State University in Mississippi rioted. The students were protesting the Kent State killings as well as racism. Most Jackson State students were African American, and were often harassed by white people driving through campus.

The rioting students overturned a dump truck and set fires. Firefighters and 75 state troopers and city police arrived at the university. Members of the Mississippi National Guard also arrived, but their weapons held no ammunition. The firefighters put out the blazes and left.

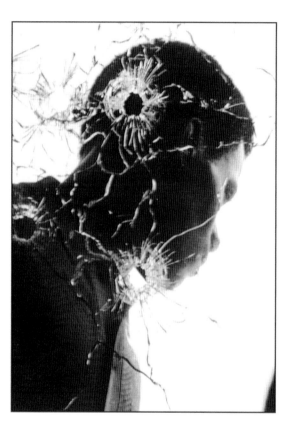

A man walks behind a shattered window in Alexander Center.

Police officers and state troopers did not leave. They marched toward Alexander Center, a women's dormitory. No one knows why. Some people threw bricks.

Then a loud noise rang out. It might have been the sound of a bottle breaking. At the same time, an item struck an officer. The police and troopers believed someone was shooting at them. They opened fire. Two students were killed, and another twelve were wounded.

The President's Commission on Campus Unrest investigated the shootings. But no one was ever charged in connection with the violence.

Portage County prosecutor Ronald Kane. Murphy wrote Kane a memo detailing which guardsmen could be charged.

Before Kane could call a grand jury, however, the fact that six of the guardsmen could be charged was leaked to the press. After a great deal of media attention, the case was passed on to the state of Ohio. Ohio attorney general Paul Brown assigned three prosecutors to the case, and a state grand jury was called.

In the meantime, the President's Commission on Campus Unrest began making its own report. At the end of its investigation, the commission concluded that the shootings at Kent State were "unnecessary, unwarranted, and inexcusable."

The state of Ohio seemed to feel differently. In October 1970, the Ohio grand jury issued a report. This report condemned the students, the faculty, and the police department at Kent State for the shootings. The jury also charged 25 people, who were mostly students but also one professor. They were charged with such crimes as arson and riot. No guardsmen were charged.

Public outrage followed the report. It was soon discovered that the jury had gone out of its way to protect the guardsmen, and it had ignored many pieces of evidence. One of the three prosecutors in charge of the case also gave a statement that bothered many people. In an interview, prosecutor Seabury Ford said that all of the protesters should have been shot on May 4. The grand jury report was later ordered destroyed by U.S. district judge William Thomas. He let the charges against the 25 listed in the report stand, however.

The President's Commission on Campus Unrest was headed by former Pennsylvania governor William Scranton.

JUSTICE

After the state grand jury disaster, the Kent State case returned to the U.S. Justice Department. But the department was still reluctant to act. Indeed, President Nixon and others were pressuring the Justice Department to do nothing. Faculty, students, and family members at Kent State tried for months to get the Justice Department to call a U.S. grand jury. Despite a petition with 10,000 signatures, the department continued to say no. Many gave up hope of a jury ever being held, though several dedicated individuals kept trying.

Then several events occurred that gave the Kent case new life. The Justice Department received a new attorney general and a new head of the Civil Rights Division. Both of these individuals were open to taking on the Kent State case. Also, a House of Representatives subcommittee had told the Justice Department that it would look into the reasons for closing the Kent case.

But the most important development was the Watergate scandal. On June 17, 1972, five men broke into the headquarters of the Democratic National Committee. The headquarters was located in the Watergate complex in Washington DC. The men were caught and arrested.

It was later revealed that these men were connected to the Committee for the Re-election of the President. The committee was

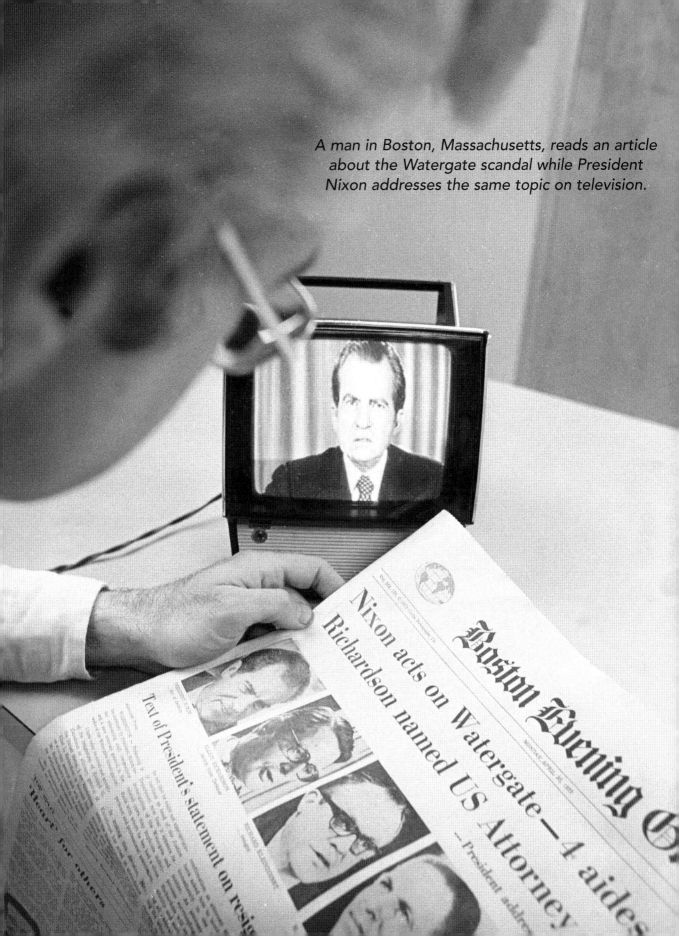

A man in Boston, Massachusetts, reads an article about the Watergate scandal while President Nixon addresses the same topic on television.

connected to Nixon, and the president suffered political embarrassment because of the incident. He also lost the respect of the public and the Justice Department. The Justice Department no longer felt it necessary to obey the president's wish to keep the Kent State case closed.

Nixon also won the contempt of Congress. In response to controversy over Cambodia, Congress passed the War Powers Act. This legislation limited the power of the president to make major war decisions without the approval of Congress. In January 1973, North and South Vietnam declared a cease-fire. Two years later, North Vietnam took over South Vietnam, and the country reunited under communist rule.

In December 1973, a federal grand jury was called to review the Kent State case. By this time, it had been more than three and a half years since the fatal shootings. On March 29, 1974, the grand jury charged eight Ohio National Guardsmen with violating the civil rights of the Kent State victims by shooting them. The specific right the jury listed was the right to due process. This meant that the guardsmen had not allowed the victims to have a fair trial before shooting them.

The eight guardsmen's trial began on October 29, 1974. In early November, Judge Frank Battisti dismissed the charges against the guardsmen. He did not believe that there was sufficient evidence to convict them. Battisti also suggested that the state of Ohio hold a trial for the guardsmen instead.

Parents and students were upset about the ruling. The state of Ohio had not pursued a trial against the guardsmen in the past. It was for this reason that the case had been brought to the federal

*Seven of the eight accused National Guardsmen
walk across the Kent State campus.*

government in the first place. Nevertheless, the parents and students
continued to pursue justice.

Six months after the criminal charges were dismissed, the
guardsmen became the target of a civil trial. Parents of the four
dead students and the nine wounded students brought a case
against the guardsmen for injuries and wrongful deaths. The civil
suit accused Governor Rhodes, Kent State University president
Robert White, and the commanding officers of the guardsmen of
wrongdoing.

It had taken more than five years for the civil trial to be held, even
though lawsuits had been filed as early as 1970. This was because

until 1974, it had been illegal to sue an agent of the state unless that person gave consent. None of the people charged with the Kent shootings had ever agreed to be sued, so the trial could not go forward. Then, on April 17, 1974, the U.S. Supreme Court decided that consent was not necessary to hold a trial. The Kent State civil trial proceeded in May 1975.

On August 27, the parents and students lost their case. In addition, the judge ordered them to pay $72,000 for court expenses. The parents and students appealed the court's decision. On September 12, 1977, a court of appeals ordered a retrial. This time, the American Civil Liberties Union (ACLU) provided lawyers to the parents and students and covered trial expenses.

The second trial began on December 19, 1978. Within a few weeks, the state of Ohio reached a settlement with the victims and the victims' parents. The parents and students would drop all charges. In return, the state of Ohio gave the parents and victims $675,000. Dean Kahler, who had been paralyzed from the waist down, received $350,000 for his injury. The other eight families each received between $15,000 and $42,000. The guardsmen and Governor Rhodes also signed a statement of regret.

Although no one has ever been found guilty for the May 4 shootings, the incident has left a lasting impression. Colleges all over the United States have created small memorials to the victims. At Kent State, the shootings have been remembered every year on May 4 with a vigil since 1970.

The nine wounded and four dead are also remembered at Kent State in the May 4 Site and Memorial. This monument was dedicated on

THE VICTIMS OF KENT STATE

Below are the four students who died in the May 4 shootings at Kent State University. William Schroeder and Allison Krause were 19. Jeffrey Miller and Sandra Scheuer were 20. Miller and Schroeder were majoring in psychology, Scheuer in speech therapy, and Krause was studying art history. Krause and Scheuer were honor students, and Schroeder was second in his ROTC class.

William
Schroeder

Allison
Krause

Jeffrey
Miller

Sandra
Scheuer

May 4, 1990. It spreads over two and a half acres (one ha) overlooking the university Commons.

The site is made up of five black disks, a wall, and four pylons made of granite. An odd-shaped plaza symbolizes conflict. The four pylons and four of the black disks represent the four students killed on May 4, 1970. They are placed near each other. Grounded farther away, the fifth disk symbolizes the fact that the tragedy had an effect beyond Kent State. The memorial is surrounded by 58,175 daffodils, one for each American lost in the Vietnam War.

At the entrance to the plaza are the words *Inquire, Learn, Reflect.* These words encourage visitors to consider what happened at Kent State, to learn from the many events that took place at that time, and to reflect on how conflict might be resolved differently in the future.

Dean Kahler, paralyzed in the shootings, sits near the May 4 Marker, the first of many memorials at Kent State dedicated to the shootings. The B'nai B'rith Hillel Jewish Services Center at Kent donated a plaque to the university because three of the four slain students were Jewish.

The plaque was placed in Prentice Lot in 1971. However, it was stolen within two years. Dr. John Ohles and other Kent faculty members were able to get the plaque replaced in 1975. Other memorials on campus include windows, sculptures, and the large May 4 Site and Memorial.

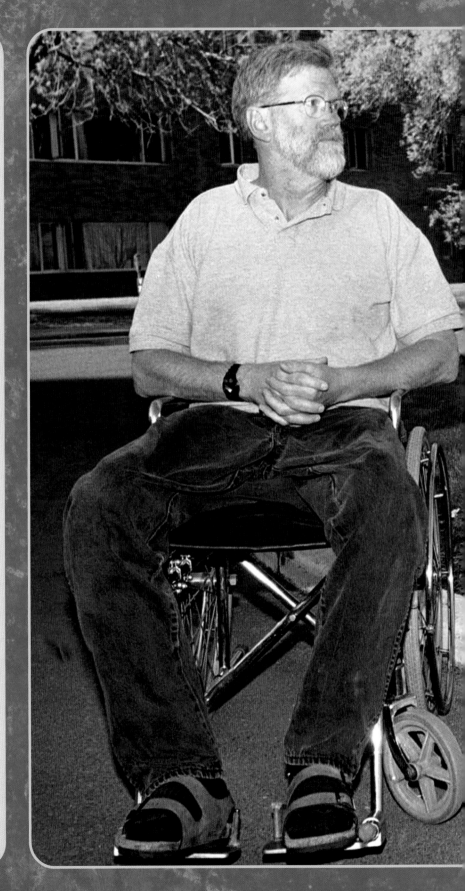

TIMELINE

1955 to 1975 The Vietnam War is fought between North and South Vietnam. The United States sends troops and advisers to help South Vietnam.

1969 President Richard M. Nixon states that U.S. troops will begin withdrawing from South Vietnam. Six months later, he calls for the first of four draft lotteries.

1970 On April 30, Nixon announces the invasion of Cambodia.

On May 1, Kent State University students hold a peaceful rally to protest the U.S. invasion of Cambodia. A riot takes place on North Water Street in Kent, Ohio, that night.

On May 2, students hold another rally, which leads to the burning of the campus Reserve Officers' Training Corps (ROTC) building. Mayor LeRoy Satrom calls in the Ohio National Guard to maintain control.

At 8:00 PM on May 3, another rally takes place at Kent State. Students become violent when guards try to end the rally and several students are stabbed with bayonets.

On May 4, a noon rally turns deadly at Kent State when guardsmen open fire into a crowd of students. Four students are killed and nine others are wounded.

Students protest the Kent State shootings at hundreds of universities across the United States. Many universities close.

In June, the Federal Bureau of Investigation (FBI) completes an investigation of the Kent State shootings. Attorney Robert Murphy of the U.S. Justice Department recommends that eight guardsmen be charged with violating the protesters' civil rights.

In October, an Ohio grand jury blames the Kent State police, students, and faculty for the Kent State shootings. The jury also charges 24 students and one professor with such crimes as arson and riot. A judge later orders the jury's report destroyed.

1972 On June 17, five men break into the headquarters of the Democratic National Committee in the Watergate complex in Washington DC. This sparks the Watergate scandal.

On March 29, a federal grand jury charges eight Ohio National Guardsmen with violating the civil rights of the Kent State victims.

In November, Judge Frank Battisti dismisses the charges against the guardsmen.

1975 In August, the Kent State victims and parents lose a civil suit against the guardsmen and various others involved in the shootings. The parents and victims are ordered to pay $72,000 in court expenses.

On September 12, an Ohio court of appeals orders a retrial of the civil suit.

The Kent State victims and their families settle the case out of court. They are awarded a $675,000 settlement for the shootings.

1990 On May 4, the Kent State May 4 Site and Memorial is dedicated.

American Moments

FAST FACTS

More than 100 American campuses closed after the Kent State tragedy because their students went on strike. The strike continued at these campuses from the day of the tragedy until the end of the school week. By the end of the week, the strike had grown to include about 80 percent of universities in the United States.

About 175,000 university faculty members protested the Kent State shootings and joined students in a strike. By the end of the strike, more than 5 million American students had participated.

Protesters of the Kent State tragedy burned a total of 30 Reserve Officers' Training Corps (ROTC) buildings nationwide by May 16, 1970. Over 35,000 National Guardsmen were called to duty in 16 states to contain the rioting.

Neil Young wrote the song "Ohio" shortly after the Kent State shootings. The song is based on the Kent incident. Because the song puts blame on President Richard M. Nixon for the shootings, it was banned from some radio stations. The song became a kind of anthem for protesters.

As a result of the Watergate scandal, President Nixon resigned on August 8, 1974. He left office the following day. Vice President Gerald R. Ford succeeded him as president. Ford gave Nixon an unconditional pardon for his role in Watergate that September.

WEB SITES
WWW.ABDOPUB.COM

Would you like to learn more about the Kent State tragedy? Please visit **www.abdopub.com** to find up-to-date Web site links about the Kent State tragedy and other American moments. These links are routinely monitored and updated to provide the most current information available.

Ohio National Guardsmen stand guard at Kent State.

GLOSSARY

bayonet: a blade fixed to the barrel of a rifle. Bayonets are used in hand-to-hand combat.

bullhorn: a handheld device that serves as a microphone and loudspeaker.

canister: a can-shaped container made to hold a specific substance.

civil rights: the individual rights of a citizen, such as the right to vote or freedom of speech.

civilian: a person who is not a member of the military.

commons: an open area that receives public use.

communism: a social and economic system in which everything is owned by the government and given to the people as needed.

conspiracy: a joining together of two or more people to commit a crime. Conspiracy is also used to describe an evil act that seems to have been planned.

controversial: something that has or can result in a disagreement.

disperse: to break up or spread out.

draft lottery: a process in the United States where men between the ages of 18 and 26 are selected for military service based on randomly chosen birth dates when a draft is in effect.

lawsuit: a case brought to court because of a perceived wrong.

leaflets: pieces of paper with words or pictures giving people information.

plaza: a public square or open area, often with trees, shrubs, and places to sit.

pylon: a towerlike structure.

riot act: a piece of legislation that bans rioting. When one "reads the riot act," that person is reminding a crowd that there is a law against gathering to disturb the peace. Those who do not leave when a riot act is read can be arrested.

sit-in: a kind of protest where people sit on chairs, on the floor, or on the ground and refuse to leave.

vandalize: to damage or destroy.

INDEX